Disclaimer

Sebastian Gray, © 2019 – All Rights Reserved

© Sebastian Gray, 2019

No part of this e-book may be reproduced, stored, or transmitted in any form or by any means including mechanical or electronic without prior written permission from the author.

While the author has made every effort to ensure that the ideas, statistics, and information presented in this eBook are accurate to the best of his/her abilities, any implications direct, derived, or perceived, should only be used at the reader's discretion. The author cannot be held responsible for any personal or commercial damage arising from communication, application, or misinterpretation of information presented herein.

All Rights Reserved.

Table of Contents

Disclaimer 2

Chapter 1: Getting the Hang of Workspace 5

    1.1 Create Documents 6

    1.2 Artboards 11

    1.3 Safe Mode 13

Chapter 2: Let's Begin Drawing 16

    2.1 Drawing Fundamentals 16

        2.1.1 Path 17

        2.1.2 Direction Lines and Points 19

        2.1.3 Modes for Drawing 20

    2.2 Pixel- Perfect Art 20

        2.2.1 Alignment of Existing Objects 21

    2.3 Working with the Pen Tool 23

        2.3.1   Straight Line Segments 23

        2.3.2   Curves 24

2.4 Working with the Curvature Tool 25

2.5 Working with the Pencil Tool 27

2.6 Basic Shapes and Lines 28

    2.6.1 Straight Lines 28

    2.6.2 Arcs 29

    2.6.3 Spirals 30

    2.6.4 Grids 31

    2.6.5 Squares and Rectangles 33

    2.6.5 Ellipses 34

    2.6.6 Polygons 35

Chapter 3: Adding Life into Drawings with Colors 37

3.1 Color Adjustments 37

    3.1.1 Equivalence of an Out-of-Gamut Color to a Printable Color 37

    3.1.2 Change a Color to a Web-Safe Color 37

    3.1.3 Blend Colors 38

    3.1.4 Modify a Color to Its Complement or Inverse 38

    3.1.5 Change the Tint of a Color 39

Conclusion 39

Chapter 1: Getting the Hang of Workspace

Adobe Illustrator is a software application used to create artwork and illustrations on a MacOS or Windows PC. It has been around since 1987 and over the years, it has evolved to become of the primary tools for graphic designers, web designers, professional illustrators, and visual artists. It is used to design printed and digital images including logos, graphs, diagrams, charts, cartoons, and illustrations. Users can also import photographs and trace any detail on it. In this way, they can end up with a sketch-like appearance of that photograph.

As a beginner, before drawing or painting, you must learn the basic controls of the Illustrator.

To create edit and files and documents while incorporating windows, bars, and panels, you can use a **workspace**.

- All the workspace elements are grouped together in a single, unified window known as **application frame**. Resizing any of its elements or the window itself generates a relative response from each of them, eliminating the possibility of overlapping.
- The **Application bar** rests at the top. It consists of application controls like menus and workspace switcher.
- You can use the **Tools panel** to create and modify artwork, images, page elements, and others.
- For the selected object, you can work around the display options in the **Control panel**.

- Your file is displayed in the **Document window**; you can divide your files in tabs. In some cases, your files can be grouped and docked as well.
- **Panels** allow users to edit and monitor their work. They can be docked, stacked, and grouped.

1.1 Create Documents

While creating a new document in Illustrator, you can select from multiple templates – stock illustrations and assets that you can add in your project. These templates end up with ".ai" extension like any other Illustrator documents; hence, it is easy to edit them according to your preferences.

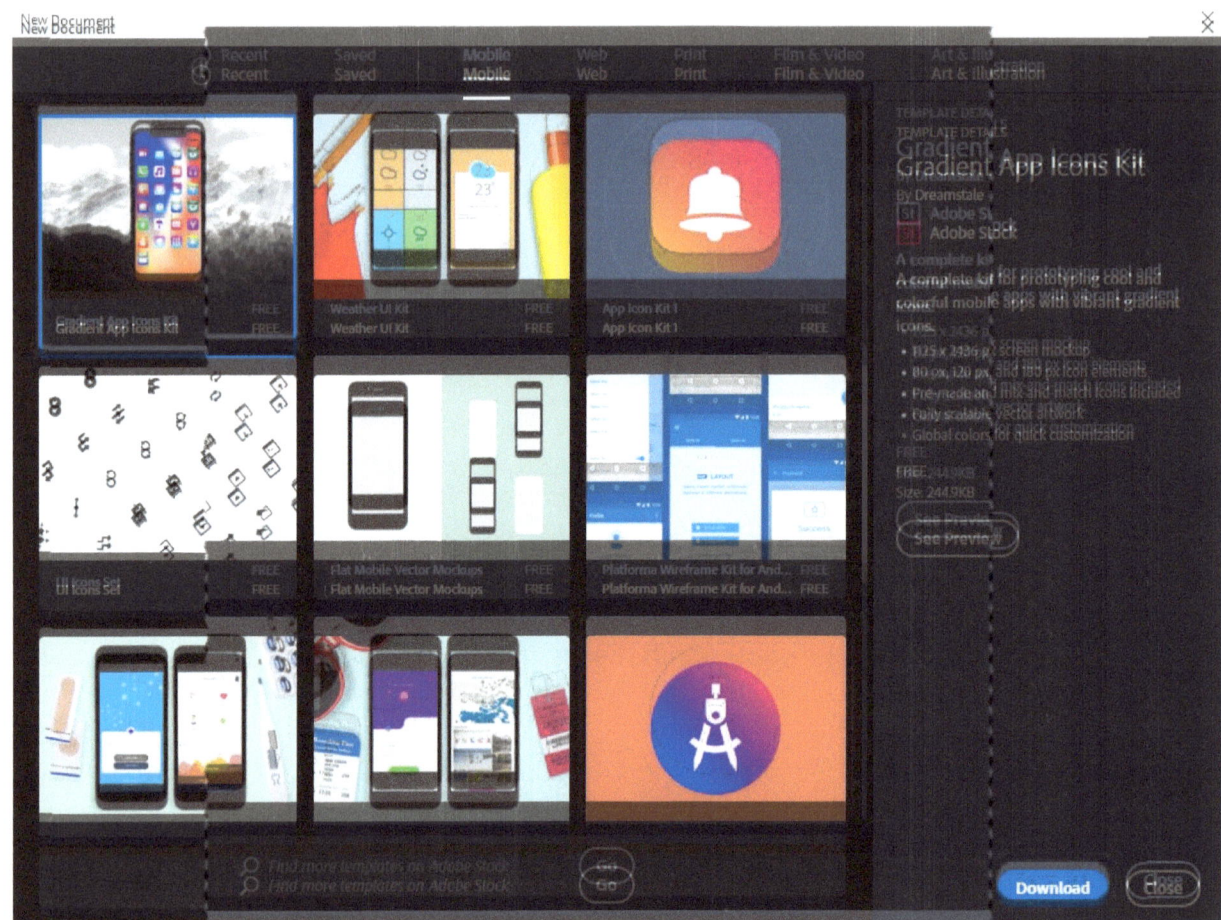

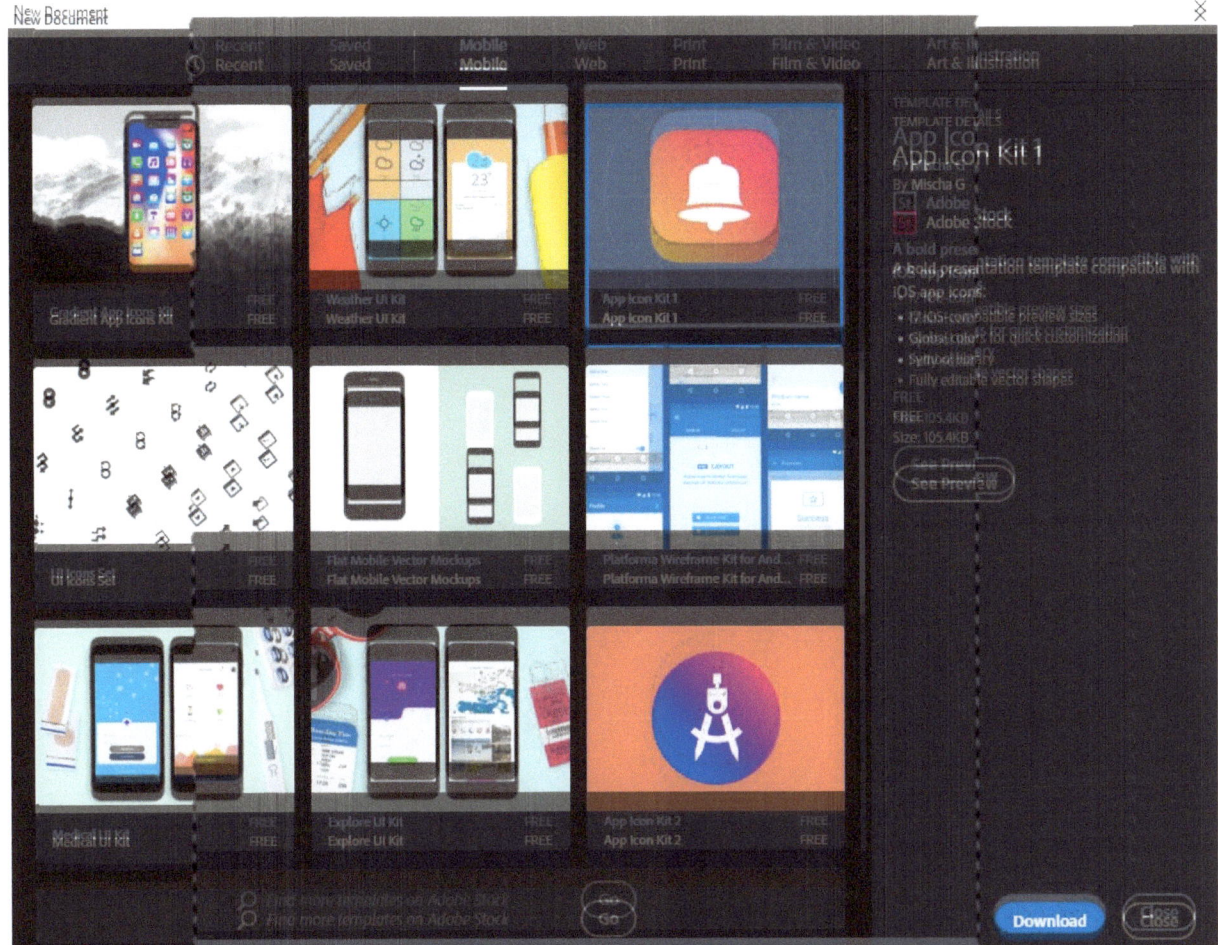

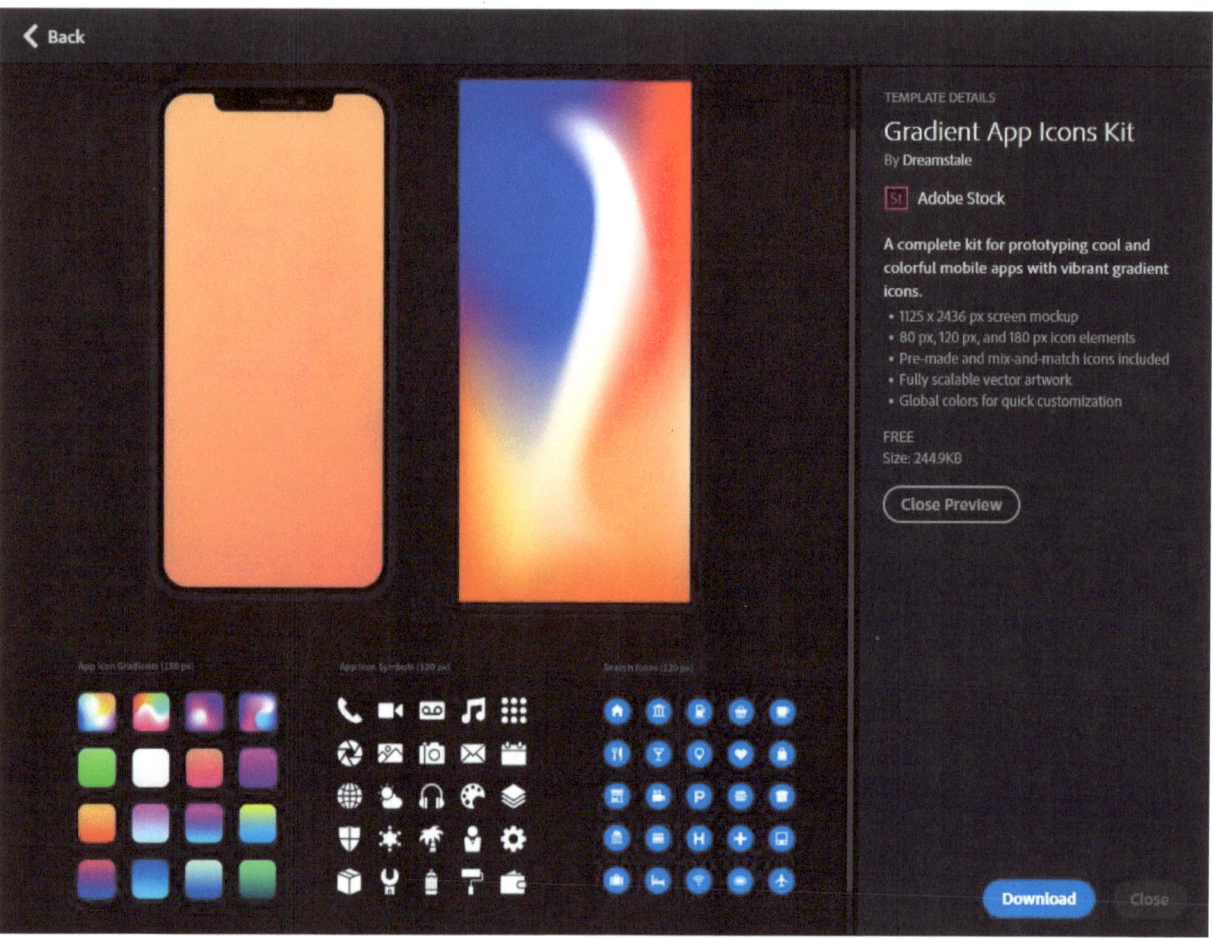

To create documents from Adobe Stock, consider the following tips.

1. Open the **New Document** dialog. Now, choose a category tab from either of the following:

    Art & Illustration, Film &Video, Mobile, Print, and Web.

2. Decide a template.

3. View **See Preview** and get an idea of how your template will appear.

4. Hit the **Download** button.

Properties Panel

You can view and edit the current workflow or tasks in the Properties panel.

1.2 Artboards

You can streamline design processes with an artboard. It provides a region where you can construct designs for various screens and devices. It signifies an area that stores exportable or printable artwork.

You can make as many as 1,000 artboards as per your requirements.

How to Create an Artboard?

1. Click on the **Artboard tool** and move it to the relevant document to set your location, size, and shape.
2. You can work with a preset artboard by double-clicking the Artboard tool. Specify a preset and choose your settings in the dialog box. Now, move the artboard to your desired position.
3. Choose the Artboard tool and click the one that has to be duplicated. Next, go to the Control or Properties panel and hit the New Artboard button. Now, keep on hitting the **Alt button** and click at the same time to generate multiple duplicates. An easier way is to select the Artboard tool and **Option + drag** in the macOS and press the Alt button on Windows.
4. Click **Esc** or select another tool from the Tools panel to get out of the artboard.

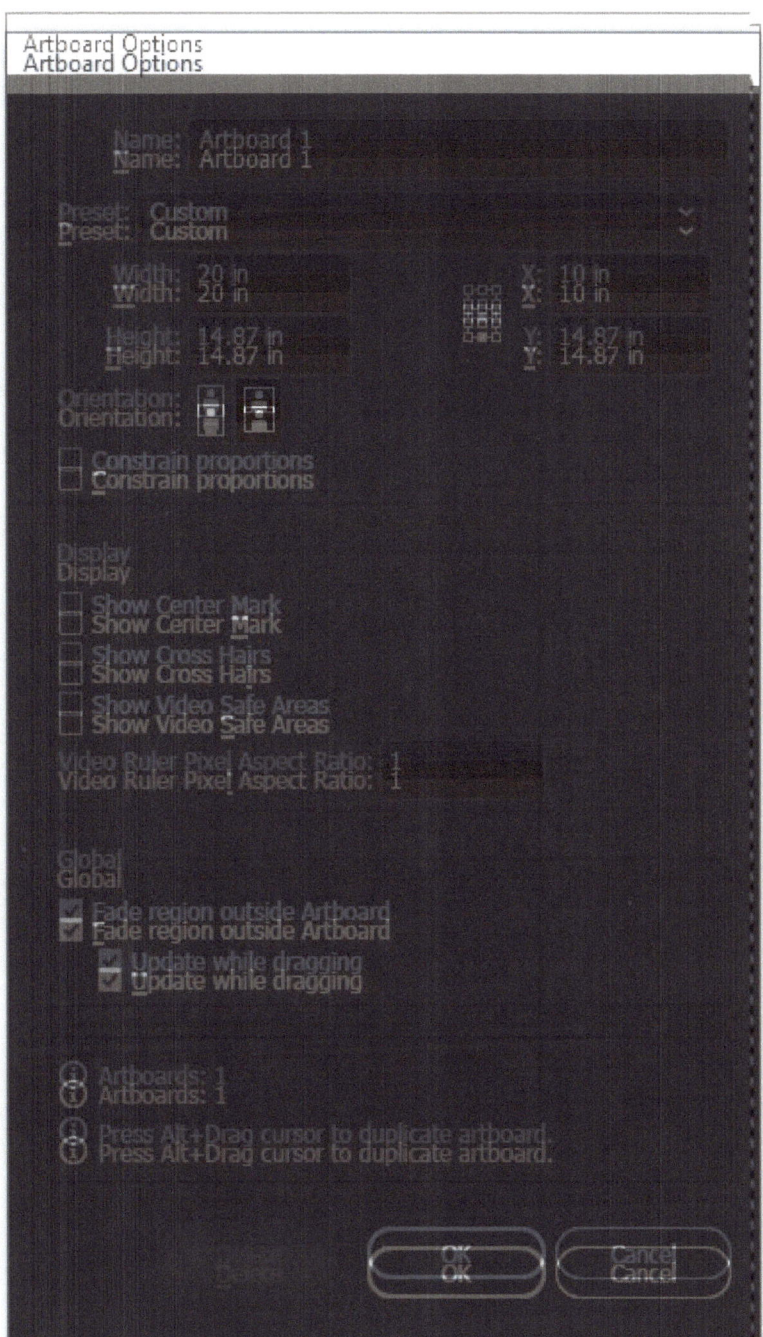

Artboard options

You can edit **Artboard Options** by double-clicking on the Artboard tool. These options include the following options:

- **Name** – Set the artboard name.
- **Preset** – Set the dimensions of the artboard.
- **Width and Height** – Set the artboard size.
- **X and Y: Position** – Set the artboard position relative to the workspace rulers in Illustrators. Go to **View → Show Rulers** to check these rulers.
- **Orientation** – Set landscape or portrait orientation
- **Constrain Proportions** – Maintains the artboard's aspect ratio if it is resized.
- **Show Center Mark** – Presents a dot in the artboard's center.
- **Show Cross Hairs** – Presents cross lines at each side of the artboard.
- **Show Video Safe Areas** – Presents guides marking the regions that belong to the video's viewable area.
- **Video Ruler Pixel Aspect Ratio** – Sets the video rulers' pixel aspect ratio.
- **Fade Region Outside Artboard** – Presents a darker shade over the area existing outside the artboard.
- **Update While Dragging** – Maintains a darker shade to the region outside the artboard when it is dragged for resizing the artboard.
- **Artboards** – Shows the number of existing artboards.

1.3 Safe Mode

In the previous versions of Adobe Illustrator, whenever a crash occurred; it was hard to diagnose the exact details that caused it. Hence, often users struggled to repair these issues. In Adobe Illustrator 2019, you don't have to worry about these bugs anymore, thanks to the Safe Mode feature. It facilitates users to diagnose and troubleshoot errors and fix them with effective repairs. Other than identifying the cause of a crash, it stops the loading of specific files and displays all those issues that are hindering the performance of Adobe Illustrator. In this way, it empowers the Illustrator to function even when it is inconvenienced by a bug – an advantage that was not available in the older versions.

How to Use Safe Mode?

Consider that your Illustrator is working fine at the moment. Now suppose, you have:

1. Launched the software. If it identifies an error-ridden or corrupt file, then your software terminates in the event of a crash.
2. In **Windows,** you can click on the **Relaunch** button whereas, in Mac, you can select the **Reopen button.** Now, Illustrator reboots.
3. Select **Run Diagnostics** and click on the **Safe Mode.** Click on the **Launch Illustrator** option to run Illustrator once more.
4. Keep in mind that this step may have to be repeated continuously. As the software is being restarted, you can find the error along with the cause – can be plug-in, driver, or font issue. This error is disabled so it does not affect the launch of Illustrator.

The following step is performed for all error-causing files. Bear in mind that interrupting diagnostic tests can cause issues.

5. After all the crash-inducing files are isolated via diagnostic steps and their information is recorded, Safe Mode initiates.

6. As Illustrator starts, you can view buggy drivers, fonts, and plug-ins.

7. Now you can either fix the errors. Or continue using Safe Mode where your buggy files remain disabled.

Chapter 2: Let's Begin Drawing

Now that we have some idea of the Adobe Illustrator environment, we can now proceed with basic drawings:

2.1 Drawing Fundamentals

Before we begin drawing, it is necessary to understand **vector graphics**. Vector graphics involve vectors – mathematics objects or shapes that create images via geometric characteristics. These vectors help in drawing lines and curves in Adobe Illustrator.

What makes vector graphics unique is that it does not lose clarity or detail, thanks to its resolution-independent property where even with resizing, they maintain the crisp edges of the drawings. This is why vector graphics are preferred to create artwork that will be customized with different output media and sizes.

2.1.1 Path

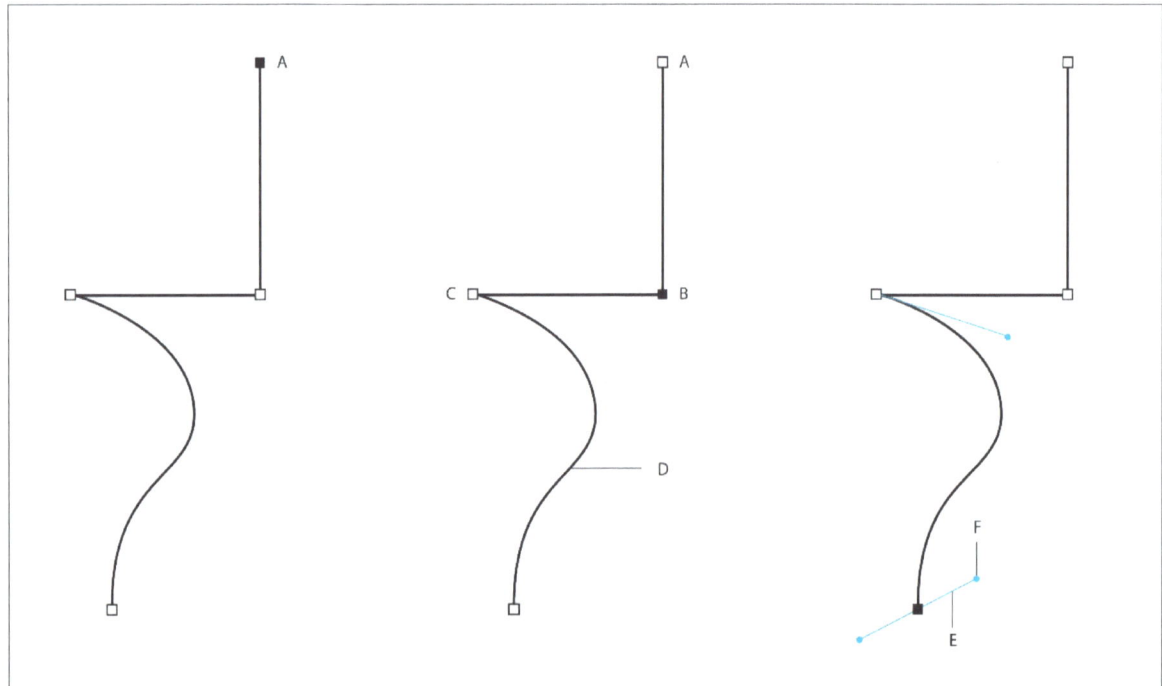

Path with anchor points

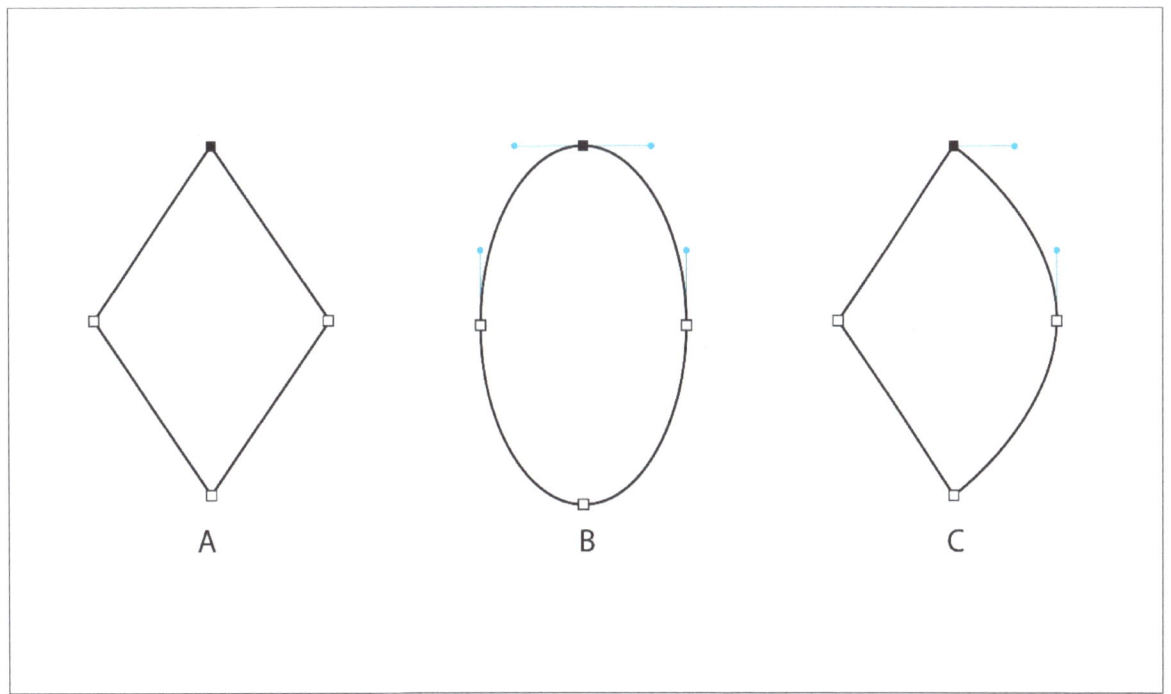

A Path with four corner points, **B** Path with four smooth points, **C** path with corner and and smooth points

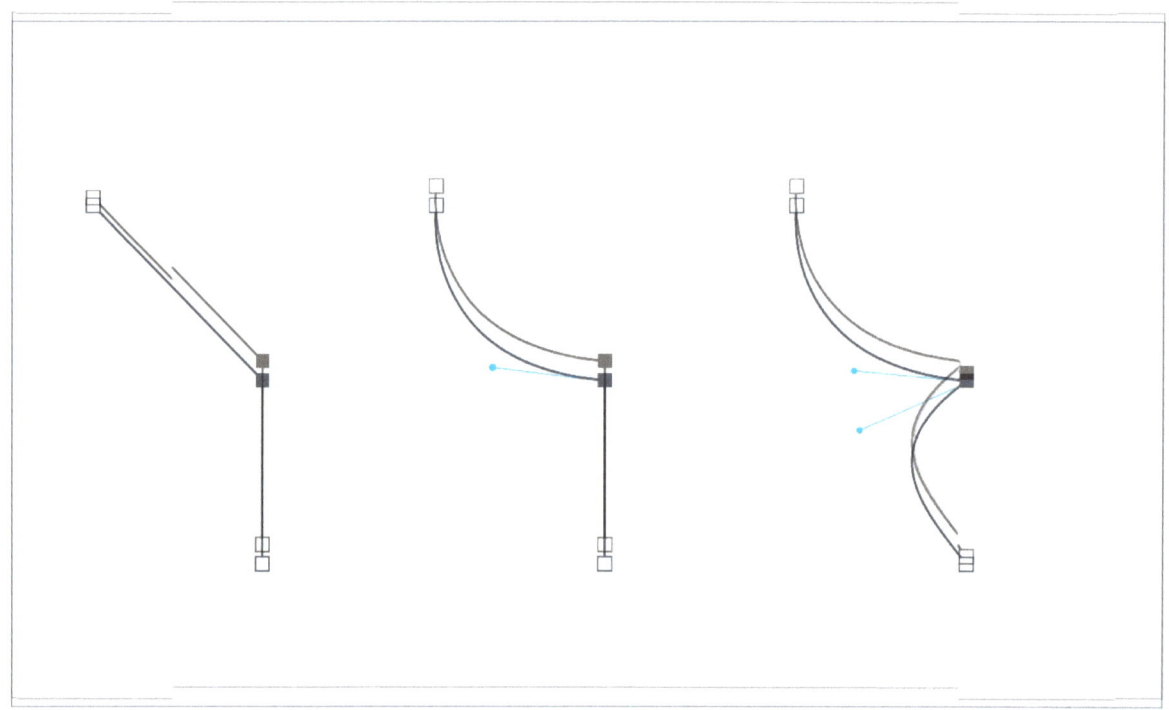

Both curved and straight segments can be linked with a corner point.

When you will start drawing, a line is generated along the way – it is known as a **path**. A path consists of a single or multiple curved or straight segments. Their starting and ending point is marked via anchor points. You can make a path open or closed (e.g. a circle). You can drag the anchor points of a path to alter its shape.

There are two types of anchor points in paths: smooth and corner points. The smooth point connects segments in the path as a continuous curve while in a corner point, it adjusts direction abruptly.

A **stroke** is the outline of a path. A gradient or color that is used for the interior of an open/closed interior region is known as a fill.

2.1.2 Direction Lines and Points

After you choose an anchor point that links curved segments, you can observe the direction handles on the anchor points. These handles contain **direction lines**, which culminate in **direction points**. The size and shape of the curved segments can be modified by changing the length and angle of the direction lines. Similarly, you can move the direction points for reshaping the curves.

If you want to hide these direction points, direction lines, or anchor points, you can go to **View → Show Edges** or **View → Hide Edges**.

2.1.3 Modes for Drawing

There are three modes of drawing in Adobe Illustrator: Draw Normal, Draw Behind, and Draw Inside. By default, you draw via the Draw Normal mode. To change mode, you can go to the Tools panel and choose from any of the modes in the Drawing Modes panel.

Draw Behind Mode

In this mode, you can draw behind all artwork with a chosen layer if there is no selection for any artwork. When an artwork is picked, the newly-drawn object is created at the bottom of the chosen object. Use this mode if you have to design new layers, place symbols, or use the File menu for file placement.

Draw Inside Mode

In this mode, your drawing occurs "inside" the chosen object. It is useful as you don't need to engage in successive tasks such as when you draw and adjust the stacking order.

2.2 Pixel- Perfect Art

With Illustration, you can build pixel-perfect art that appears crisp and clear-cut on all screens.

To do this, you have the flexibility to utilize various stroke alignment and width options.

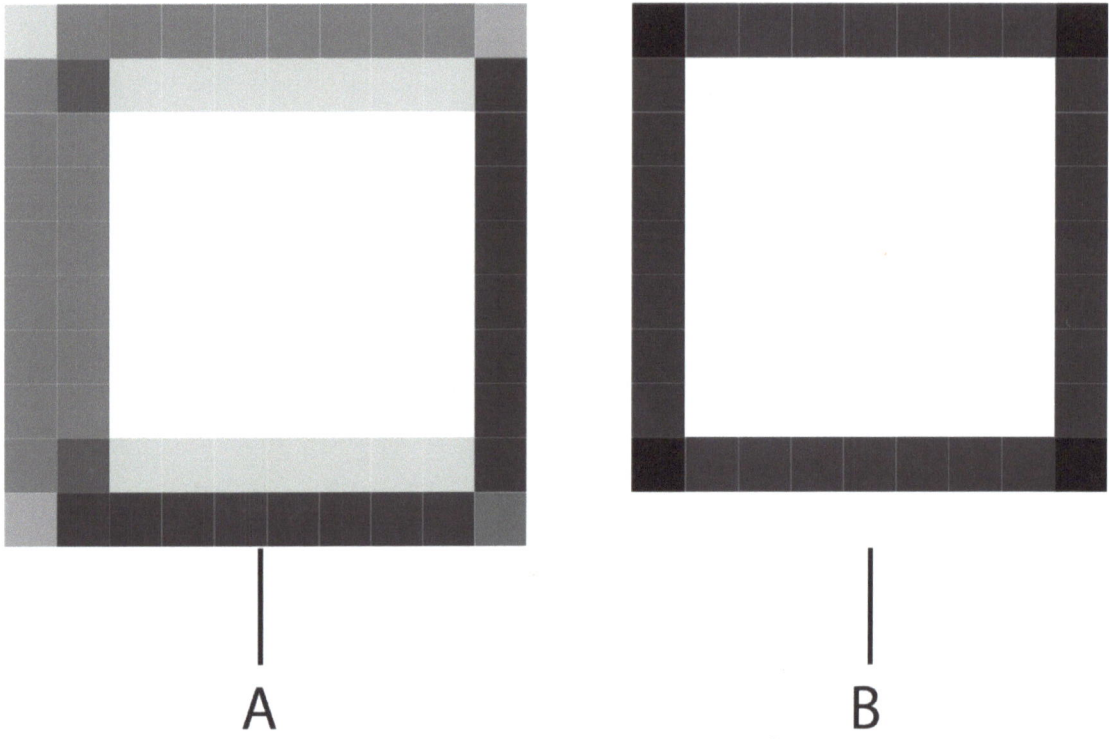

An Object is not aligned according to the pixel grid. B Object is aligned according to the pixel grid.

2.2.1 Alignment of Existing Objects

You can pick from object segments or objects that are currently stored in your existing art and align these existing objects with the pixel grid.

1. Choose the **Selection** tool to choose the existing object for alignment with the pixel grid. If you have to choose a specific object segment, then utilize the **Direct Selection** tool.
2. In order to transform an existing object as pixel perfect, perform the following tasks.

- Go to the control panel and hit the **Align Selected Art to Pixel Grid** button.
- Select **Object→Make Pixel Perfect.** By right-clicking it, go to the in-content menu and select **Make Pixel Perfect.**

Align Transformed or New Objects

To make up for accurate edge and path placements while generating or transforming objects, you can perform the following actions.

1. Choose **View → Snap to** Pixel. Alternatively, go to the Control Panel and hit the **Align Art to Pixel Grid on Creation and Transformation** button.
2. You can also go to the drop-down menu and adjust the setting to **Snap to Pixel**. Hit the arrow icon and go through a **Pixel Snapping Options** dialog for adjustments.
3. Hit the **OK** button.

To examine the pixel grid, choose **View → Pixel Preview.** Now, zoom on the canvas and increase magnification to 600%.

2.3 Working with the Pen Tool

2.3.1 Straight Line Segments

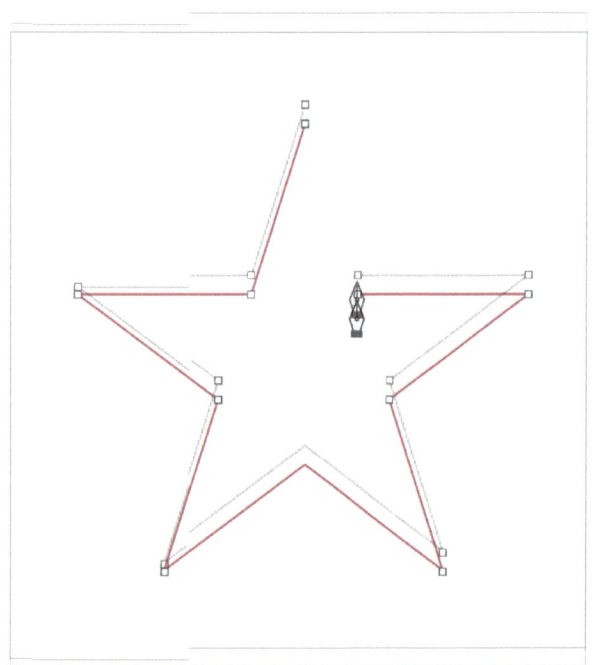 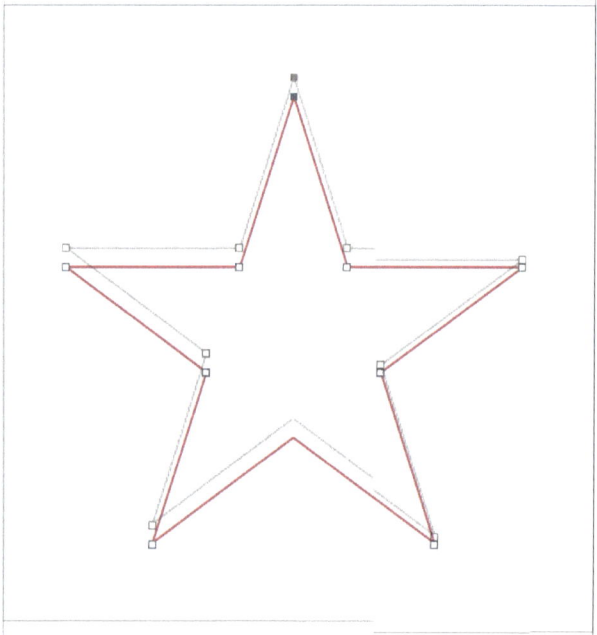

A star is drawn with the Pen tool

Straight lines are the simplest to draw. Click the **Pen** to generate a pair of anchor points. As you keep clicking, a path consisting of straight line segments is drawn, where corner points link the drawing. Here is a step-by-step procedure to create straight line segments.

1. Choose the **Pen** tool.
2. Choose any position on the screen where you would like to draw on the screen. Click that to specify your beginning anchor point.
3. Next, pick another spot and click the Pen tool again – this is where your line segment from the previous step ends.

4. Repeat these clicks and specify further anchor points to make your drawing of straight-line segments.

5. To finish the path, apply any of the following:

- For an open path, Command-click (macOS) or Ctrl-click (Windows) at any spot that is far from other objects.
- For an open path, you can pick **Select → Deselect** or simply choose another tool.
- For a closed path, take the tool back to the initial (it will be hollow) anchor point. If positioned correctly, a little circle emerges around the **Pen** pointer. Close the path via dragging or clicking accordingly.

2.3.2 Curves

To make curves, add an anchor point at the spot where your curve alters direction; you can shape the curve by dragging the direction lines. The curve shape relies on the slope and length of the direction lines.

1. Choose the Pen tool.
2. Choose any position in the screen where you would like to draw the curve on the screen and press down the mouse button until the initial anchor point emerges and an arrowhead form is taken by the pointer of the Pen tool.
3. To adjust the curve slop, drag the pointer and release the mouse button.
4. Place the Pen tool at the spot that you would like as the endpoint of the curve segment. For instance, if you want a curve in the form of a "C" letter, drag the pointer opposite to the previous direction line, after which you can release the mouse button.

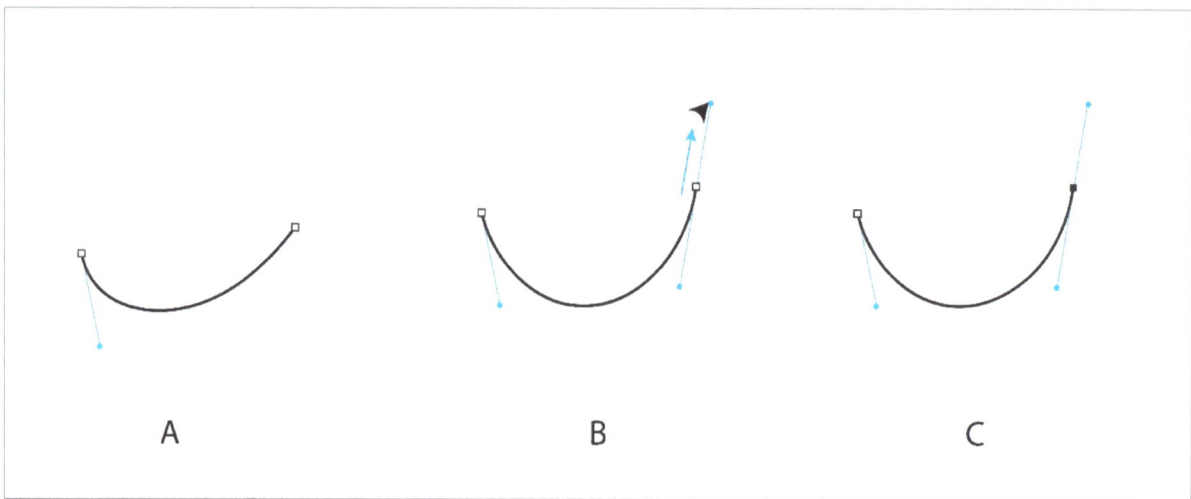

Creating the second point of a curve

5. Keep dragging the Pen tool to generate multiple smooth curves in various locations.

6. To finish the path, perform the following.

- For an open path, Command-click (macOS) or Ctrl-click (Windows) at any spot that is far from other objects.

- For an open path, you can pick **Select → Deselect** or simply choose another tool.

- For a closed path, take the tool back to the initial (it will be hollow) anchor point. If positioned correctly, a little circle emerges around the **Pen** pointer. Close the path via dragging or clicking accordingly.

2.4 Working with the Curvature Tool

The **Curvature** tool is commonly used to ease up the creation of paths. It infuses a valuable touch of intuitiveness and convenience in drawings. You can use it to add, edit, toggle, and create corners and smooth points. Following is a brief example of how you can use this tool.

1. Choose the Curvature tool.

2. By dropping two points with the artboard, you can check the preview of the rubber band. It shows the resulting path in terms of shape, relying on the hovering of your mouse.

3. Drop a point with the mouse to generate a smooth point. Double-click to generate a corner point.

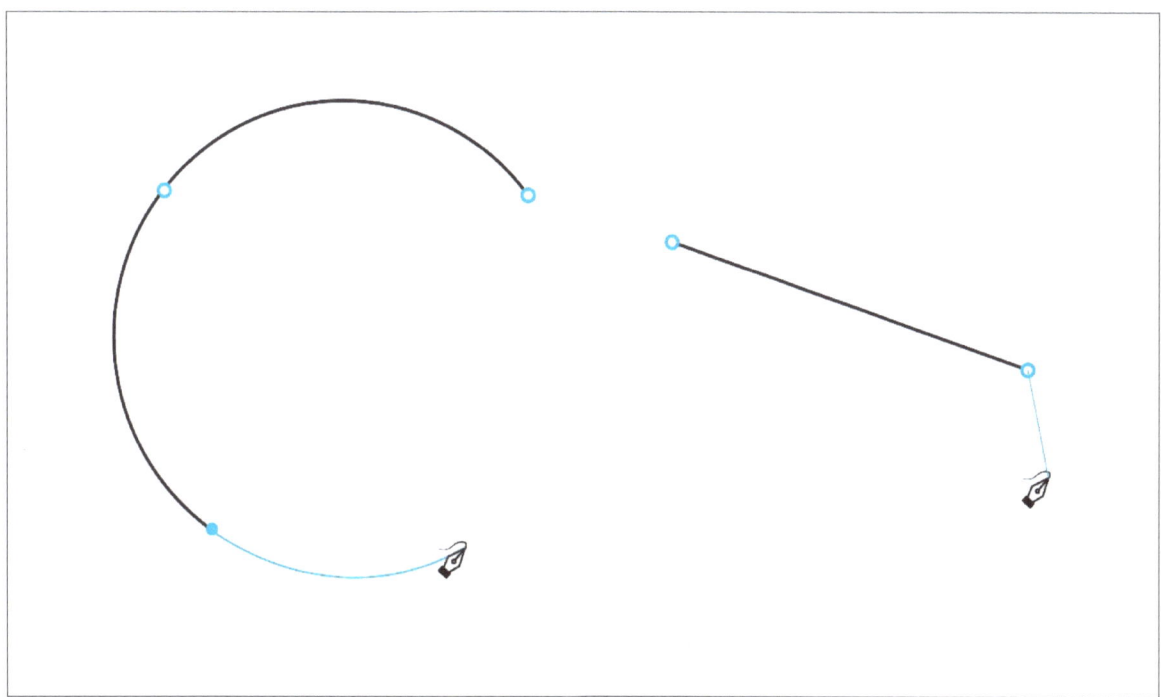

A Smooth points are drawn by default B Double-click to create a corner point

4. There is a variety of actions to take part in with the tool. Some of these are:

- Alt (Windows)/Option (macOS) + click for continuing with the addition of points to an existing shape or path.

- Double-click a point and toggle between the corner and smooth points.

- Select a point and move it by dragging it.

- Select a point and delete it by pressing the Delete button. In this way, the curve is maintained.
- You can stop drawing by pressing the Esc key.

2.5 Working with the Pencil Tool

The Pencil tool allows designers in drawing open and closed paths with the same ease they do it with a pencil. Use this tool if you are short on time for fast sketching. After drawing a path, it is easy to modify it when required.

To draw freedom paths, follow these steps:

1. Select the shaper tool and choose the **Pencil** tool.
2. Position the tool to a spot from where the path should begin, and drag to draw it. A little "x" appears to reflect the formation of a freeform path with the Pencil tool.

In order to draw unconstrained straight segments, press the Alt/Option key for drawing unconstrained straight segments. To plot a polyline path, apply these steps:

1. Create a line segment.
2. Hold the mouse button, release, and hit the Alt/Option and Shift key, so you can draw the succeeding segment.

To draw constrained straight segments, press the Shift key and apply the Pencil tool for drawing straight segments. These can be constrained to 90, 45, or 0 degrees. During this drawing, you can see the straight-segment cursor.

2.6 Basic Shapes and Lines

2.6.1 Straight Lines

With the line segment tool, you can create one single line segment at a time. Consider these steps:

1. Choose the **Line Segment** tool.
2. Engage in any of the following:

- Pick a location from where the line should begin, take the pointer there and drag to the ending point of your line.
- Click at any spot from where the line should begin. Go to the dialog box, set the **Angle** and **Length** of the segment.

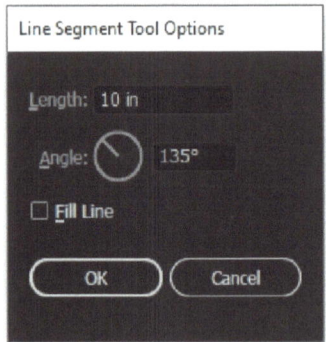 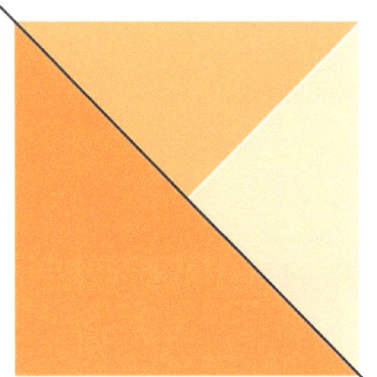

options in the Line Segment tool

2.6.2 Arcs

1. Select the **Line Segment** tool, hold it, and choose the **Arc** tool.

2. Perform any of the following actions.

- Pick a location from where the line should begin, take the pointer there and drag to the ending point of your line.

- Now think about the beginning point of the arc. Go to the dialog box and from the reference point locator, select a square. Afterward, you can adjust options like Type, Base Along, Fill Arc, Slope, and then click OK.

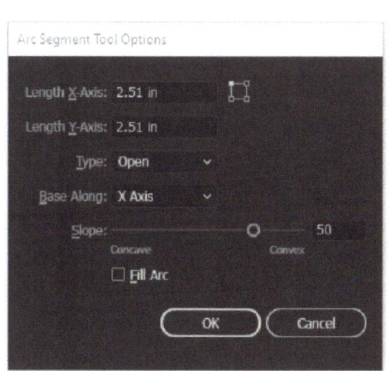

Options in the Arc Segment tool

2.6.3 Spirals

1. Select the Line Segment tool and choose the **Spiral** tool.

2. Consider any of the following options.

- To draw the preferred spiral, keep dragging the Spiral tool. For rotation, you can drag the pointer with an arc.

- Click the spot where the spiral has to be drawn. Choose the following options in the dialog box and click OK:

    o **Radius –** Sets the distance from the spiral's outmost point to its center.

    o **Decay –** Sets the amount for which all spiral winds have to be reduced.

    o **Segments –** Sets the number of segments in a spiral.

    o **Style –** Sets the spiral's direction.

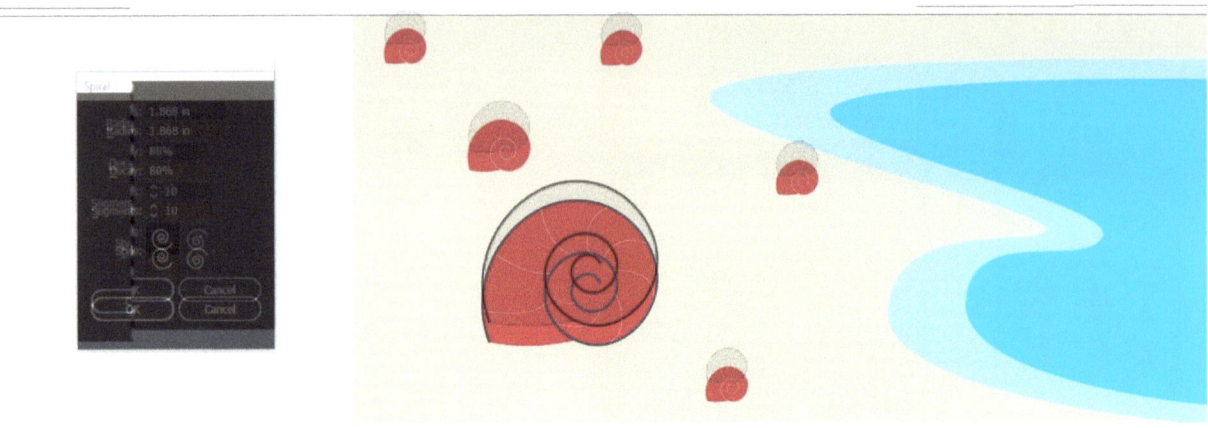

Options in the spiral tool

2.6.4 Grids

Grid tools are used to draw polar and rectangular grids quickly. The Polar Grid tool is used to design concentric circles for any size and dividers. Similarly, the Rectangular Grid is used to build rectangular grids of the preferred size and divider.

To draw a rectangular grid, follow these steps.

1. Go to the Line Segment tool → Rectangular Grid Tool.
2. Now using the Rectangular Grid tool, apply the following steps.

- Until the grid gets the intended size, keep dragging it.
- Click and specify the reference point of the grid. Select a square from the reference point locator in the dialog box and calculate the point on which the grid has to be drawn. Afterward, consider the following options and hit the OK button.
    - Default size
    - Vertical dividers

- Horizontal dividers

- Fill grid

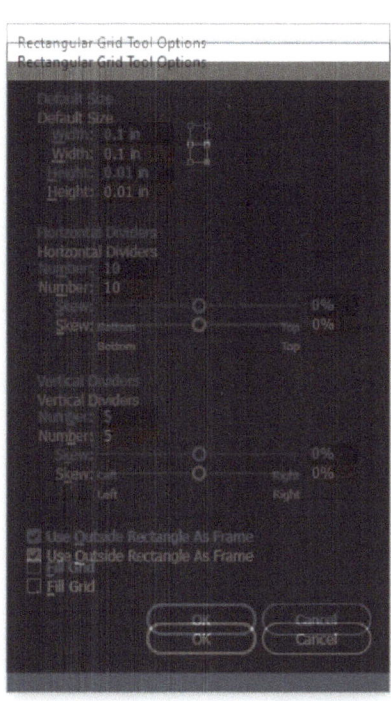
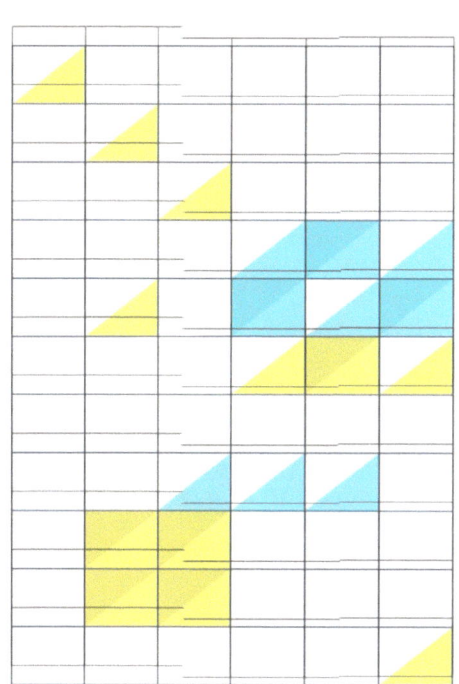

Options in the Rectangular Grid tool

On the other hand, follow these steps to draw polar grids.

1. Go to the Line Segment tool → Polar Grid Tool.

3. Now using the Polar Grid tool, apply the following steps.

- Until the grid gets the intended size, keep dragging it.

- Click and specify the reference point of the grid. Select a square from the reference point locater in the dialog box and calculate the point on which the drag has to be drawn. Afterward, consider the following options and hit the OK button.

- Default size
- Concentric dividers
- Radial dividers
- Fill grid

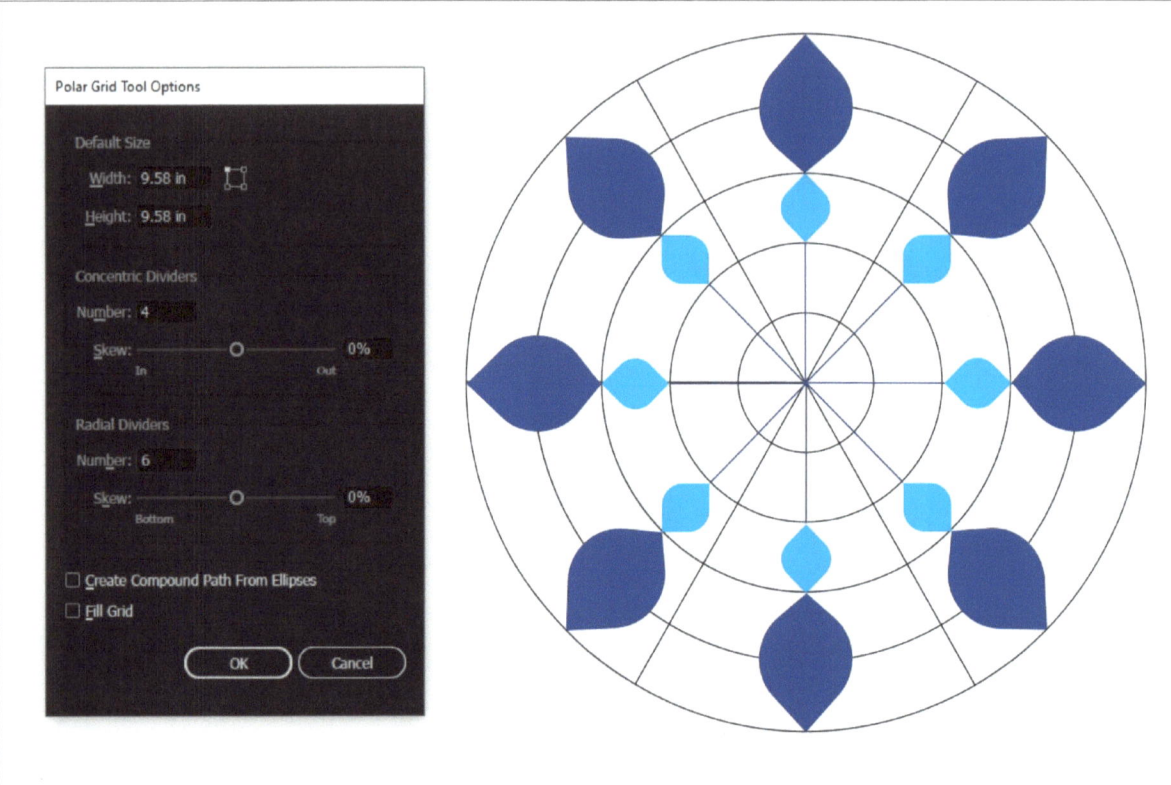

Options in the polar grid tool

2.6.5 Squares and Rectangles

1. Choose the **Rounded Rectangle** or **Rectangle** tool.

2. Perform any of the following actions.

- To produce a rectangle, drag the tool diagonally in a bid to set up the preferred dimensions.

- To produce a square, press the **Shift** key and drag the tool diagonally in a bid to set up the preferred dimensions.

- To use values for producing rectangles or square, go to the top-left corner and specify a height and width.

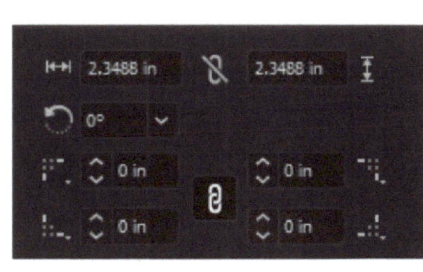 

2Options in the Rectangle tool

2.6.5 Ellipses

1. Select and press the Rectangle tool and choose the **Ellipse** tool.

2. Perform any of the following actions.

- Drag the tool in a diagonal trajectory until a preferred size is reached for the ellipse.

- Select a point in the top-left corner for the bounding box of the ellipse. Similarly, set a height and width for the ellipse.

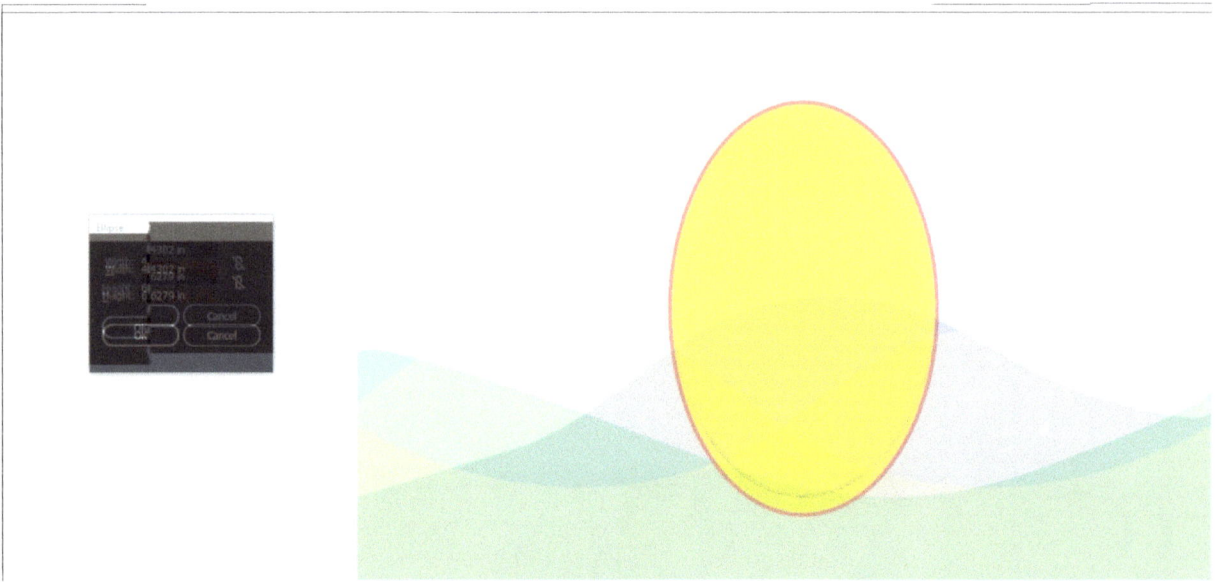

Options in the Ellipse tool

2.6.6 Polygons

1. Select and press the Rectangle tool and choose the **Polygon** tool.

2. Perform any of the following actions.

- Drag the tool in a diagonal direction until a preferred size is reached for the polygon. For polygon rotation, drag the pointer in an arc. Arrow keys from the keyboard like **Up** and **Down** can be used for the management of the polygon, such as for adding and removing sides in it.

- Choose a spot as the polygon's center. Now, set a fixed number of polygon sides and assign a radius to it.

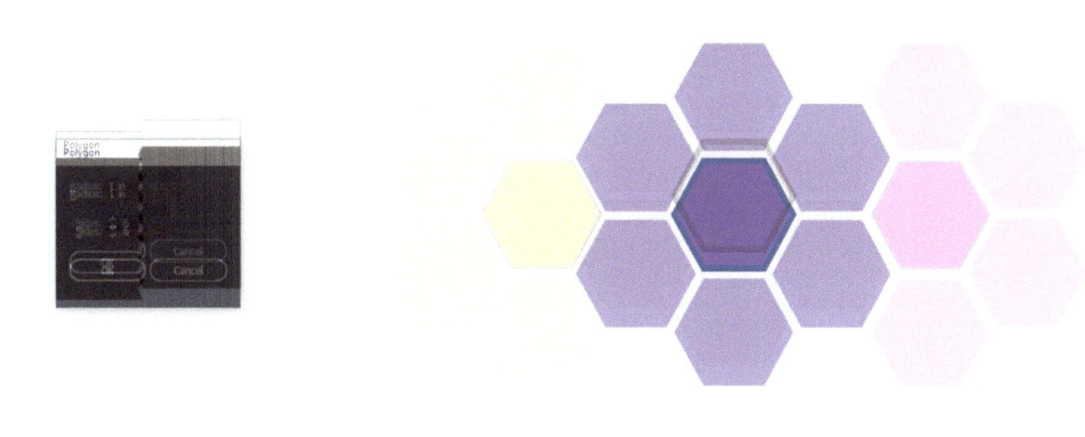

Options in Polygon tool

Chapter 3: Adding Life into Drawings with Colors

In Adobe Illustrator, it is a fairly common practice to apply colors to different artworks. However, it must have some ideal color modes and models.

Color models point to those colors that are used in "digital" graphics. They have several types like HSB, CMYK, and RGB – each of them shows a unique method to describe and categorize color. They compute numerical values to delineate the color spectrum. Color models include a variant known as color space that includes certain ranges of colors.

3.1 Color Adjustments

3.1.1 Equivalence of an Out-of-Gamut Color to a Printable Color

In HSB and RGB color models, not all colors are printable, such as neon colors. This is due to the lack of a corresponding equivalent in the CMYK model. If you are in such a predicament and you choose an out-of-gamut color, you will notice an alert triangle in the Color Picker or Color panel. To address this issue, select the triangle and shift to the nearest equivalent of the CMYK model. It is shown in a tiny box along the triangle.

3.1.2 Change a Color to a Web-Safe Color

All browsers use web-safe colors – around 2016 colors. In case you don't use a web-safe color, an alert cube can appear in the Color Picker, Color panel, Edit Colors.

Now, click the cube to go to the lowest web-safe color (represented by a small box along the cube).

3.1.3 Blend Colors

The Blend commands form up a string of intermediate colors that are taken from a group of 3 or more filled objects. It calculated the horizontal or vertical orientation of a project. Blending does not have any impact on unpainted objects or strokes.

1. Choose three or more filled objects.
2. Perform any of the following.

- Edit → Edit Colors → Blend Front to Back (fills blends between frontmost and backmost filled objects)
- Edit → Edit Colors → Blend Horizontally(fills blends between rightmost and leftmost filled objects)
- Edit → Edit Colors → Vertically(fills blends between topmost and bottommost filled objects)

3.1.4 Modify a Color to Its Complement or Inverse

1. Pick any color that you would like to modify.
2. Go to the Color panel and pick an option from the panel menu.

- If you choose **invert**, it transforms all the color components to the exact opposite value mentioned in the color scale. For instance, if an RGB color has a R value of 50, then by applying invert command, it will change 205 (255 - 50 = 205).

- If you choose **complement**, it transforms all the color components to newly-generated value that comes from the addition of the lowest and the highest RGB values.

3.1.5 Change the Tint of a Color

1. In the Swatches panel, choose a global spot color or process color.
2. Enter a value in the textbox or drag the T slider in the Color panel to adjust the intensity of the color. The range of the tint begins from 0% and ends at 100%; lower number lightens the tint.
3. For saving the tint as a swatch, click the New Swatch button from the Swatches panel. In this way, it is saved, using the same name as the name of the color. For instance, if you have saved color called "Navy Green" at 30 percent. If you save it as a swatch, then it will be named as "Navy Green 30%."

Conclusion

Up until now, you have covered enough ground to be called as a beginner in Adobe Illustrator 2019. You know how to:

- Use the workspace effectively.
- Create basic drawings.
- Color your drawings.

After practicing these chapters thoroughly, you can easily catch up to the more advanced concepts of Adobe Illustrator and create breathtaking, dazzling designs from scratch.

www.ingramcontent.com/pod-product-compliance
Lightning Source LLC
Chambersburg PA
CBHW051934210526
45473CB00006B/2246